Bev Schneir # Marin Revealed **Glynis Mariani**

For Paul and Trish's friends
Connie and Jon –
Enjoy the book!
Glynis Mariani

SKYLIGHT EDITIONS

San Rafael, California
info@skylighteditions.com

Published by SkyLight Editions
San Rafael, California
e-mail address: info@skylighteditions.com

Manufactured in Hong Kong

Library of Congress Cataloging in Publication Data
Library of Congress Control Number: 2002093882
Marin Revealed
Photography
Schneir, Bev and Mariani, Glynis.
Includes:
English language text
Preface
Kenna, Michael.
Foreword
Allende, Isabel.
Essay
Sharett, Deirdre.
Plate annotations.
Bibliographical references.

ISBN: 0-9721452-0-6

Design by Lise Stampfli Torme, San Anselmo, California
Printing by Global Interprint, Inc., Santa Rosa, California

First Edition October 2002
front cover: Plate 77 *Journey, St. Vincent Drive*
foreword plate: *Spirit Rock*
back cover: Plate 20 *Dark Clouds, Approaching Marin*

CONTENTS

PHOTOGRAPHERS' STATEMENT

Often we are asked to identify a particular image as belonging

to one or the other of us. But that is a difficult thing to do. Although

ultimately only one of us released the shutter on any individual photograph,

this collection is a truly collaborative effort. Together we journeyed out to

explore the secluded corners of Marin, discover different perspectives on

its more familiar landscapes, and reveal what we found through the camera's

lens. This book is our personal interpretation of a place we love, a

place of incomparable beauty, a place we know as home.

Glynis Mariani & Bev Schneir

PREFACE
Michael Kenna

The distinguished photographer Ruth Bernhard often gives her students an exercise: to photograph within a few feet of their beds in order to better appreciate the "gift of the commonplace" in one's immediate surroundings. Many photographers have taken Ruth's wise words to heart and among them I would count Beverly Schneir and Glynis Mariani. They have moved further afield than Ruth's initial suggestion, but have stayed true to the principle of photographing in their own neighborhood, Marin County, California, which they obviously know very well.

If you are looking for a guidebook to Marin County with digitally enhanced, full color pictures of the popular tourist spots, *Marin Revealed* is not the book for you. The ninety photographs you will find on these pages portray a Marin that frequently goes unnoticed by most of us city dwellers who make occasional brief forays across the Golden Gate Bridge. This is a very personal Marin, seen through the perceptive eyes of two women who live there, and have a deep connection to their surroundings. These images invite us all, locals and outsiders, to share in their admiration for this particular corner of the earth.

Photography allows us to edit and examine fragments of time from the continuum of life. Eugene Aget, who photographed around Paris for over thirty years, demonstrated that nothing is ever the same twice, and Beverly and Glynis attest to that. Returning to their locations over a period of two years, they witnessed both dramatic and subtle changes: trees fell, new buildings sprang up, seasons moved on and weather shifted. The infrared and fast speed films that Beverly and Glynis chose to use rendered what they photographed in a somewhat surrealistic way. For these and other reasons, we would not see the same scenes in exactly the same way on our own journey through Marin.

Wandering through this collection of quiet images is like going for a delightful Sunday afternoon walk with two good friends. We feel special being shown unfamiliar yet cherished corners of the landscape, intimate places that are both well loved and often visited by our guides. The walk has both a soothing and almost dreamlike quality to it. These photographs slow us down, displace us from our fast paced lives, and become catalysts for our daydreams. They challenge us to pay more attention to the underlying beauty that surrounds us, and they remind us that life rushes by and the important things seem to disappear much too soon.

Michael Kenna, a master of black and white photography, has been photographing the landscape for nearly three decades. His work has been shown in numerous exhibitions throughout the United States, Europe, Asia, and Australia. Kenna's work is included in such permanent museum collections as The National Gallery, Washington, D.C., The Victoria and Albert Museum, London, and The Bibliotheque Nationale, Paris. His many books include *Michael Kenna —A Twenty Year Retrospective, The Rouge, Le Notre's Gardens, Night Work, Impossible To Forget,* and *Easter Island.*

Spirit Rock

FOREWORD

Isabel Allende

The most important events of my life have occurred without much planning. Life takes its own course in spite of me. Coming to live in Marin County was one of those surprising turns of fate that have marked my journey in this world. It all started in 1987, during a hectic book tour for one of my novels, maybe the third one. San Francisco was the last city on the trip and the only one where I stayed for three days, so there was a chance for some sightseeing. Somebody had organized the usual Chinatown—Muir Woods—Napa Valley excursions for me, but the program changed at the last minute because something unexpected happened: I met a man. William Gordon, an attorney who had read one of my books, decided to show up at one of the readings. I liked him immediately. Also, I had been chaste for a very long time—two or three weeks, as I recall—so I accepted a bit too promptly his invitation to show me around. Marin County was the place where he had been living for the previous twenty years, after traveling over most of the world. I was exhausted and frankly more interested in him than in the natural beauties of this area which I didn't expect to see again.

Willie picked me up at the hotel in San Francisco in his car, filthy with stale fries and fur all over the seats—soon enough I learned that he had a child and a dog—and we headed toward the Golden Gate Bridge, which I had seen in movies and on postcards. Nothing had prepared me, however, for the spectacle of a bridge suspended in the air from two proud red structures that looked like ancient Chinese war towers. On the left side was the Pacific Ocean, an open invitation to the vastness of the Orient and those mysterious places frequented by the likes of Marco Polo. To the right was the bay, much larger than I had imagined, sprinkled with white sails. Hundreds of elegant seagulls flew above us while tourists and joggers crossed the bridge challenged by the chilly autumn wind.

"Some people travel from afar to jump from this bridge. It makes sense to end one's life with style," Willie commented casually.

As we drove north the landscape turned into something comparable to the Cote d'Azur in France, only better. Willie took me along a winding road all the way up Mount Tamalpais. It was a cool October day and the sky was so clear that from the top we could see all the Bay Area extended like a magnificent tapestry at our feet. The voluptuous curves of the hills, the deep mirror of the water, and the dark shadows of the woods, seemed almost unreal, like a watercolor. It was one of those rare moments of epiphany, when we are hit by the flash of an insight or the sharp premonition of things to come. The beauty of the scenery took my breath away and suddenly I had tears in my eyes. There was nothing to say, because language was irrelevant. How can words describe a vista so stunning that it hurts? Granted, I was tired, but let me assure you that I am not the kind of person that weeps easily. Willie pretended not to notice. He probably thought that he was stuck with an emotionally unstable Latin female and he'd better get rid of her as soon as possible. He pointed out and named the towns of Marin County one by one, like the beads of a rosary.

He explained to me that most of Marin County had developed slowly until the Golden Gate Bridge was built, when it became a suburb of San Francisco. Only twenty minutes away from the stress, the temptations, the crowds and the excitement of the city, Marin County seems like another world altogether. He talked about the feeling of space and freedom that it provides, about the slower pace of life, which allows the body to relax and the spirit to grow.

Sausalito, the first city north of the bridge, used to be a workingman's town, full of gambling dens and brothels, where ships were made until after the Second World War. Little did we know at that moment that a few years later both of us would be working in one of those houses of ill repute. Wait a minute, it doesn't sound right, does it? The Victorian house where Willie has his law office and I have my studio is not a brothel today, but it has the prestige of having been the first one in Sausalito. It was also a Christian church, a chocolate chip cookie factory, and then it was divided into a bunch of small shops until it fell into our hands in 1990. It has gone down in the social scale, but the perfume of the madams, the incense of the Sunday services, and the sweet aroma of cookies still linger in those rooms. Many benevolent spirits live in that house.

After showing me the view from the top of Mount Tam, Willie gave me a tour of the county. First we visited the houseboats and quaint shops of Sausalito. I noticed the tourists gathering in large groups around the ferry, people reading in coffee shops or walking their dogs, bikers all over, women with their kids in strollers. At first sight it seemed like a movie set, too clean and lovely to be real, but in the weeks to come I learned that it is absolutely so. I also noticed several modest beach houses that were selling for the price of a small castle in Scotland!

We headed north on the freeway to have coffee in Mill Valley, an enchanting town where many artists and writers have chosen to live. On the square young people with spiky purple hair, nose rings and roller skates were playing chess, while a blind woman played the guitar and sang ballads like a Medieval damsel. On the wall of a store there was a puzzling sign: *No perfume or deodorant allowed in consideration of the scent challenged.*

"Mill Valley is the capital of the politically correct folks," my host said. I had never heard that expression and it has no translation in Spanish, maybe because the concept does not exist elsewhere.

Then we drove to Tiburon to see the skyline of San Francisco, the Golden Gate Bridge and the sailboats. We window-shopped along a picturesque street where Persian rugs were offered side by side with baseball caps and costume jewelry. We visited a Scandinavian bakery where we had to defend our pastries from the seagulls.

"You should take the ferry, it's a memorable experience," Willie said, but he did not offer to accompany me. Instead he decided that I needed a map and he took me to a lively bookstore in Corte Madera, where the owner greeted me effusively—she had read my books—and she didn't charge for the map. By then it was almost noon and I was wondering if I should invite this man to lunch. I didn't know how to handle it. Would he think that I was insinuating myself? I certainly hoped that he would.

We made it to Larkspur where he pointed out several restaurants, but didn't stop at any of them. Instead he went to an Italian bakery and bought sinful pastry. "For dessert," he announced. Then he drove to Greenbrae to get an organic chicken. We passed Kentfield and Ross where he showed me the splendid residences of the truly rich, hidden under luscious vegetation. We stopped in San Anselmo for a fresh baguette and a bottle of California chardonnay which, according to him, was probably the best in the world. I was too polite to contradict him. Obviously he hadn't heard about the superiority of Chilean wine. We strolled along the streets of the little town admiring the antique shops and the funky secondhand clothing stores. My budget was pitiful, but I could afford a woolen scarf. It was getting cold.

"Where are we going?" I asked, hoping to be kidnapped. "To a magic place," he replied. We passed the town of Fairfax, populated mainly by old hippies and earth mothers, and continued along a curvy road to West Marin. We were soon surrounded by the hills and patches of oak trees like the ones I'd seen from the top of the mountain. Six black buzzards were perched defiantly on a fence rail next to the road we traveled, either simply eyeing us or waiting for a better snack.

"That way is Spirit Rock, a sacred site for American Indians and a gathering place for modern spiritual seekers," Willie explained, pointing at a narrow road and to an old tree that seemed to emerge from the heart of a large rock. He added that in Marin almost everybody is into some kind of quest; those who are not in search of enlightenment are in search of the perfect tofu meat loaf. "This is the natural habitat for gurus, Zen masters, New Age fanatics, seers, prophets, and self-proclaimed goddesses. The rest of the population is into wildlife, therapy, aerobics, peacock feathers, designer water and hot tubs. On the whole, they are a compassionate and rather charming lot," he explained.

The landscape changed as we entered Samuel P. Taylor State Park and then I understood what Willie meant by a magic place. It was a world of gigantic trees, of solitude and silence. The leaves shimmered when caressed by the timid rays of the October sun; the air smelled of rich soil and humus; the only sounds were the chirping of birds and of water rushing in the creek. We parked under a grove of tall redwoods and very quietly, so as not to disturb nature, prepared our picnic. There was no one; we were the only living souls in that extraordinary green sanctuary. Willie started a fire in a stone barbecue pit, and while the chicken slowly roasted over the coals we sipped our wine in silence, wrapped in our jackets. Beams of sunlight carrying particles of dust came through the redwoods, creating the effect of a fairy tale illustration.

I have been in many, many places. As a child I wandered all over, following my stepfather who was a diplomat. In my youth I became a traveler and later a political refugee. My fate had been to move around and say good-by to cities and friends; I had no roots and thought that I would never have them. At the time I was living in exile in Venezuela, following the military coup of 1973 that ended a century and a half of democracy in Chile, my country. For a very long time I had not had a home that I could call my own, but on that day in 1987 in those ancient woods, in the company of the stranger that Willie was, I felt that I had found my place. I had the intuition that I belonged there and with that man.

We left the park when the sun was setting and the landscape had acquired an eerie appearance. Thick fog rolled in as we drove south to San Francisco and rapidly the world disappeared. The yellow lights of other cars seemed like ghosts passing at a great distance. We were alone, enveloped by whiteness and silence.

Was it then when I decided to leave everything behind and plunge fully into the adventure that lay ahead? I don't recall the exact moment, but it was certainly at some point during that first day in Marin County. Of course Willie had no idea of what was going through my mind, otherwise he would have run in the opposite direction. Like most American bachelors he was not willing to make a commitment, let alone to a short foreign woman whom he had just met. But he was no match for me. Let's say that I was able to convince him to love me in return. It didn't happen right away; it took some maneuvering on my part, but finally he surrendered and a few months later we married.

For once following my instinct was not a disaster; on the contrary, the decision I made impulsively on that first date proved to be a very wise one. In Marin County I have found love, built a home, and grown roots. I have lived here for so many years that I can hardly remember my life anywhere else. I know it well, yet it surprises me every day. Many things have not changed, although it has grown and become more crowded. We still have the sense of open space, the tranquil rhythm of life, and the freedom that one enjoys in a place that is safe and tolerant where people are respectful of each other. Nature, however, changes all the time. Every single day is different. One never tires of the scenery.

In spring newborn fawns roam the streets, seals appear on the shores of the bay, and flowers bloom all over. Marinites take out their biking gear, they go hiking, and bird or whale watching. They also place personal ads in search of a temporary companion. There are many singles in Marin, and although most would like to remain so, mating is popular in spring.

Summer is long, dry and pleasant. There is no need to go anywhere else on vacation. The beaches are full, everybody dresses in light colors and sandals, children play around in flocks, and thirsty wildlife escapes from the hills that have turned golden, looking for water in public parks and private gardens.

My favorite season is autumn, when the trees compete in their best attire and we see them in all shades from pale yellow to deep vermilion. The sky has those same colors at dawn, when the wild geese fly south. On some clear nights, when the moon is reflected on the water, I am almost sure that I have seen angels glide in the silvery light.

There is no need for a heavy coat in Marin as winters are never too cold. True fanatics go surfing in December and most of them survive the experience. I like the rare storms of thunder, lightning, wind and rain, when the waves wash over the road that leads to our house and the world seems to come to an end. Winter is a lovely season of reflection—a time for friends and family, for bookstores, art galleries, restaurants, movies, theater and music.

In a few words, let's say that Marin County is as close to paradise as you can get while still breathing. It was most fortunate that Willie lived here when I dumped myself in his lap. Thanks to him I have a home in the best possible location. Eventually I was able to bring my son and his family from Venezuela. He now lives very close to us in San Rafael. My daughter Paula died in our home and her ashes are scattered in the same park where Willie and I had our first picnic. Two of my three grandchildren were born here. When I tuck them in bed I tell them stories about mythical creatures that live in the hills, in the redwood forests, in the fog, and at the bottom of the bay.

In these years living in Marin County I have written several books and I hope to write many more in the future. Most of my friends and none of my enemies live here. My grandchildren are growing up here. On top of a hill Willie and I built our house and planted a garden where everything grows with manic speed and luscious abundance. We have a breathtaking view of Mount Tamalpais, the bay, and the surrounding hills. On a clear day we can see the skyline of Oakland and three bridges.

Willie and I have been through hell and back; we have experienced success and great losses; we have fought like crazy and made up several times, but we are still together. We come from different cultures, and really we have little in common. It always amazes me that lust would turn into love, just like it does in a cheap romance novel. I have to admit that living in Marin County has a lot to do with our happiness.

This is one of the most beautiful and peaceful areas in the world, where people still manage to live graciously. It is a place that invites us to wander around, to appreciate the changing sights, to discover the hidden corners. That is exactly what Bev Schneir and Glynis Mariani have done. For years they have captured the fleeting moods of this county which they know so well and love so much. In their evocative images the spell of Marin is revealed.

Isabel Allende is the author of many books including *The House of the Spirits, Of Love and Shadows, Eva Luna, Paula, Daughter of Fortune,* and *Portrait in Sepia.* Her works have been translated into 27 languages and have been bestsellers in Europe, the United States, Latin America, and Australia. Recipient of many honors and awards, Allende has been a resident of Marin County for 15 years.

A Delicate Feast
Deirdre Sharett

Marin County, California, is a mystical place peopled by artists and writers, hikers and bikers, wildlife lovers and conservationists, spiritual seekers, the banker, the baker, and probably the candlestick-maker. This book shows you what has drawn them here. It is an aesthetic exploration of Marin, a poetic weaving of past and present in shimmering, sensuous images. And it is an antidote to the anger, fear, and chaos of the world, a tonic to the terrible images assaulting our hearts and burned into our psyches daily by newspapers and TV screens.

From the gulls of Lime Point to the curious round pot sitting on the ground at Olompali, the book is replete with lyrical, luminous, often mysterious, images. Some, like the Tennessee Valley beach after a storm, with the stranded picnic table sitting strangely in the water, bring to mind with their grainy quality the pointillist paintings of Seurat. Piercing the darkness, eerie headlights approach us through a dreamlike stand of peeling eucalyptus trees; paths, gates, stairs, archways beckon; a meditating angel presides over the cemetery at Bolinas; an aging pier at China Camp vanishes into the mist. On one day Angel Island emerges from a meringue of fog that hugs the water, while on another, fog hovers about the top of Mount Tamalpais. And frequently a pervasive gentle fog magically softens entire landscapes, creating scenes like the seductive curves and reflections at Nicasio Reservoir. Elsewhere, the Fairfax Theatre, Old St. Hilary's Church, Pierce Point Ranch, the Old Town Novato poultry buildings, and other man-made structures stand hard-edged and clear in the ordered space between earth and sky.

From the cliffs above Rodeo Beach, we look back across black rocks and the foam-laced shore to the old barracks and military buildings that appear like a mirage in the distance. And then there are the boats: sailboats, houseboats, the circle of overturned boats at Marshall, the *Point Reyes* beached at Inverness. A lone egret stands, a sober sentinel, beneath besotted wires; deer observe us observing them; two geese walk proudly toward a pond; three cows graze casually. We still have dairies in Marin, and even vineyards.

Some of the photographs, such as the profoundly beautiful scene found on Point San Pedro Road, are simple and serene as a Zen painting, while others are complex, embracing more chaotic elements all reigned in carefully and deliberately. Photograph after photograph returns the viewer to a quiet, calm, still place. This tranquil world is offered to us in sepia tones. Without the strident distraction of color, light becomes even more important. We see the images more clearly, feel them more deeply. Light and luminosity imbue them with a spiritual quality. They shine with an incandescent intensity, haunt us with their ethereal glow.

The two photographers know well, just as philosophers do, that all is impermanent. Heraclitus told us that twenty-five centuries ago. You can't step twice in the same river. Change is the only permanence. We have seen how, in an instant, the skyline is suddenly bereft of well-known structures, the earth can rumple and rupture; or waves can batter the shoreline, as time and the seasons wear familiar landmarks away. And there is always the ongoing narrative of the changing light played out against the plots introduced by the capricious quirks of Marin's mercurial weather.

The photographers stalked the wild light to capture these images, and present them to us before they disappeared. They have used their cameras to express their passion for Marin. Walking softly on the planet, they show us what we have to lose, revealing at one and the same time the tension between the timeless qualities of nature and the all too poignant consequences of the passage of time. And at least here, between these pages, time is stopped—which is what the camera does—and it is done with abundant artistic intelligence and grace. The fleeting evanescent beauty, fragile as the melting flakes of a rare snowfall on Mount Tamalpais, can be caught by the camera's lens and the perceptive, loving eye of the photographer, so that long after the snow melts, we can all be nourished by the images captured and now reproduced in this compelling collection. It is a delicate and entirely satisfying feast, the result of the soul's need to find beauty, and the heart's need to preserve it.

Deirdre Sharett is a well-known Bay Area poet, author of *Language of a Small Space*, and contributor to numerous small press publications and anthologies. One of the founders and incorporating directors of the Marin Poetry Center, she ran a poetry reading series for seven years at the Mill Valley Book Depot.

T H E P L A T E S

Plate 1

Gateway to Marin

Plate 2

City View, Marin Headlands

Plate 3

Gulls, Lime Point

Plate 4

Rodeo Beach, Fort Cronkhite

Plate 5

Bunkers, Fort Baker

Plate 6

Two Bridges, Kirby Cove

Plate 7

Masts, Belvedere Island

Plate 8

Dawn, Point San Pedro Road

Plate 9

Suspended Walkway, Point Bonita Lighthouse

Plate 10

Morning Fog, Angel Island

Plate 11

Last Light, Point Bonita Lighthouse

Plate 12

Half Mile Pier, Point San Quentin

Plate 13

Tethered Boat, China Camp

Plate 14

Sling Launch, Marinship

Plate 15

Reflections, San Pablo Bay

Plate 16

Float Plane and Houseboats, Richardson Bay

Plate 17

Caged Bird, Muzzi Marsh

Plate 18

Three Seagulls, Net Depot

Plate 19

Winter Sky, Richmond-San Rafael Bridge

Plate 20

Dark Clouds, Approaching Marin

Plate 21

Tangled Wires, China Camp

Plate 22

Five Minutes, Bunker Road

Plate 23

Mirror Image, Larkspur Trestle

Plate 24

Fountain, Plaza Viña del Mar

Plate 25

Spillway, Alpine Dam

Plate 26

Sunlight, Muir Woods

Plate 27

Sawmill, Old Mill Park

Plate 28

Autumn Leaves, Camp Bothin

Plate 29

Campsite, Samuel P. Taylor Park

Plate 30

Snow 2001, Mountain Theatre

Plate 31

Last Stop, West Point Inn

Plate 32

Winter Picnic, Mount Tamalpais

Plate 33

Shibui, Mount Tamalpais

Plate 34

Stranded, Tennessee Valley Cove

Plate 35

Vanishing Point, China Camp

Plate 36

Raven in Silhouette, Inverness

Plate 37

Stone Steps, Old St. Hilary

Plate 38

Gazebo, Marin Art and Garden Center

Plate 39

Lyford House, Tiburon

Plate 40

Stone Arch, Montgomery Chapel

Plate 41

The Castle, San Anselmo

Plate 42

Ivy Wall, The Seminary

Plate 43

Dunphy Park, Sausalito

Plate 44

Garden Gate, Robson-Harrington Park

Plate 45

671 Steps, Dipsea Trail

Plate 46

Inkwells, Lagunitas

Plate 47

Log Shelter, Phoenix Lake

Plate 48

Glenwood Bridge, Ross

Plate 49

Falkirk, Mansion Row

Plate 50

Three Crosses, Mission San Rafael

Plate 51

Palm Trees, St. Vincent

Plate 52

Cinema, Fairfax

Plate 53

Old Town, Novato

Plate 54

County Line, Petaluma River Bridge

Plate 55

Marin County Civic Center, San Rafael

Plate 56

Siesta, Hamilton Field

Plate 57

Fallen Oak, Buck Center

Plate 58

Driving Range at Dusk, McInnis Park

Plate 59

Last Standing Gate, Olompali

Plate 60

After the Harvest, West Marin

Plate 61

Iron Pot, Olompali

Plate 62

Lone Oak, Ignacio

Plate 63

Downtown, Nicasio

Plate 64

Three Cows, Hicks Valley

Plate 65

Paradise, Blackie's Pasture

Plate 66

Windmill, Chileno Valley

Plate 67

Maine Street, Tomales

Plate 68

Shadows, Point Reyes-Petaluma Road

Plate 69

Escalle, Magnolia Avenue

Plate 70

Wooden Arbor, Green Gulch

Plate 71

Clasped Hands, Horseshoe Hill

Plate 72

Meditating Angel, Bolinas

Plate 73

Morning Mist, Marinwood

Plate 74

Elephant Rocks, Dillon Beach Road

Plate 75

White Fence, Dillon Beach

Plate 76

Solitude, Nicasio Reservoir

Plate 77

Journey, St. Vincent Drive

Plate 78

Six Curlews, Seadrift

Plate 79

Lifeguard Station, Stinson Beach

Plate 80

Low Tide, Tomales Bay

Plate 81

Boat Dock, Bolinas Lagoon

Plate 82

Promontory, Point Reyes Lighthouse

Plate 83

Circle of Boats, Marshall

Plate 84

Tower, Point Reyes Lighthouse

Plate 85

Cottage, Cypress Grove

Plate 86

Oyster Beds, Tomales Bay

Plate 87

Lifeboat Station, Chimney Rock

Plate 88

Late Afternoon, Pierce Point Ranch

Plate 89

Three Trees, Limantour Estuary

Plate 90

Day's End, Mount Tamalpais

PLATE 1 **Gateway to Marin**
The Golden Gate Bridge, designed to resist turbulent winds and earthquakes, is an engineering miracle. The suspension bridge, built under the direction of chief engineer Joseph B. Strauss, was completed in 1937. Eleven men lost their lives during the four-year construction period.

PLATE 2 **City View, Marin Headlands**
San Franciscans have flocked to Marin for many years. They first traveled by ferry to vacation and escape the fog. After the 1906 earthquake they fled the city, increasing Marin's population by sixty percent. With the opening of the Golden Gate Bridge, the number of residents grew even more dramatically.

PLATE 3 **Gulls, Lime Point**
Located at the entrance to the San Francisco Bay, Lime Point was most likely given this name because of the abundance of bird droppings. When viewed from this point, the Golden Gate Bridge is often concealed by fog, but the perpendicular rocks called the Needles remain visible.

PLATE 4 **Rodeo Beach, Fort Cronkhite**
Rodeo Beach, also known as Cronkhite Beach, was once home to the military. Former army barracks can be seen in the distance. Fort Cronkhite is now home to the California Marine Mammal Center which rehabilitates injured and abandoned marine mammals.

PLATE 5 **Bunkers, Fort Baker**
The bunkers and decaying gun emplacements at Fort Baker are part of the Golden Gate National Recreation Area and reflect the former military presence. In 1972 the federal government purchased the land for a public park, saving the property from development.

PLATE 6 **Two Bridges, Kirby Cove**
Kirby Cove, just west of the Golden Gate, was named for Lieutenant Edmund Kirby who was wounded during the Civil War. While the lieutenant lay dying, President Lincoln personally saw to it that he received a promotion.

PLATE 7 **Masts, Belvedere Island**
Called an island, but actually part of a peninsula, Belvedere is comprised of elegant homes with spectacular views and winding, half-hidden lanes. Belvedere was once named Kashow's Island for its first settler, Israel Kashow, who lived on the site where the San Francisco Yacht Club now stands.

PLATE 8 **Dawn, Point San Pedro Road**
This view from Point San Pedro Road, on the peninsula in San Rafael, is one of Marin's most scenic drives. Along the shoreline are stretches of marsh, tidelands, and bird nesting areas.

PLATE 9 **Suspended Walkway, Point Bonita Lighthouse**
The hike to the Point Bonita Lighthouse in the Marin Headlands includes a walk across a 165-foot suspension bridge. Relatives of the cabbage plants, originally grown to supplement the meager provisions provided for the keeper of California's last manned lighthouse, can still be seen growing on the sides of the steep cliffs.

PLATE 10 **Morning Fog, Angel Island**
Discovered by the Spanish explorers, Angel Island has been a refueling stop for whalers and otter hunters, a Mexican cattle ranch, an American military base, an Asian immigrant quarantine station, and a Nike missile base. It is now a California state park.

PLATE 11 **Last Light, Point Bonita Lighthouse**
Located in the Marin Headlands, the Point Bonita Lighthouse was built in 1855 near its present site, 306 feet above sea level. The tall, narrow lighthouse was often obscured by fog, making it necessary to fire a cannon every thirty minutes to warn the sailors. In 1877 the lighthouse was rebuilt on a lower site; the original top was severed and added to the new structure.

PLATE 12 **Half Mile Pier, Point San Quentin**
At 2,300 feet, this private pier situated at Point San Quentin is nearly half a mile long. In 1852 an old brig called the *Waban* was towed to this point and used to house San Quentin's first prisoners. It was the beginning of a tumultuous history that has seen scandals, violence, fires, riots, and executions.

PLATE 13 **Tethered Boat, China Camp**
China Camp is located just beyond McNear's Beach in San Rafael. This California state park was originally a debarkation and relay point for Chinese laborers. They were smuggled in by night to work on the construction of the Central Pacific Railroad.

PLATE 14 **Sling Launch, Marinship**
This Sausalito shipyard operated around the clock during World War II. Its workers built a total of 93 ships, including fifteen Liberty ships. At its peak tens of thousands of employees worked there, including women and over half of the San Francisco Symphony orchestra.

PLATE 15 **Reflections, San Pablo Bay**
San Quentin Peninsula on San Pablo Bay was named for an Indian leader whom the Spaniards called Quintin. He helped lead the last tribal resistance in Marin before being captured by soldiers in 1824.

PLATE 16 **Float Plane and Houseboats, Richardson Bay**
In the 1880's Richardson Bay, located north of Sausalito, was home to so many dismantled sailing ships that it was known as "The Boneyard." Later, the area became a resting place for abandoned ferryboats. These huge vessels were converted to living quarters and workspaces for artists and craftsmen.

PLATE 17 **Caged Bird, Muzzi Marsh**
Muzzi Marsh was dedicated to the state as a wildlife habitat and open space in 1981. There are 526 acres of marshland at the mouth of Corte Madera Creek.

PLATE 18 **Three Seagulls, Net Depot**
Located in Tiburon, the Net Depot was established by the United States Navy during World War II. The Navy planned to build a net seven miles long and weighing 6,000 tons that would stretch across the bay from Sausalito to San Francisco to keep out enemy submarines. The project was halted when Pearl Harbor was attacked.

PLATE 19 **Winter Sky, Richmond-San Rafael Bridge**
The Richmond-San Rafael Bridge, connecting the East Bay to Marin, was opened in 1956 to replace the ferry service. It is four miles long and has a double deck but no pedestrian walkways.

PLATE 20 **Dark Clouds, Approaching Marin**
This bridge, also called the San Rafael-Richmond Bridge, was designated the John F. McCarthy Memorial Bridge. It honors a man who served as a state senator for sixteen years.

PLATE 21 **Tangled Wires, China Camp**
After the railroad was completed in 1869, the Chinese workers settled on these shores and began a flourishing shrimp fishing industry. Restrictions on the type of nets used, the planting of bass, and a fire that destroyed many shanties, forced most of the inhabitants to abandon the area by 1913.

PLATE 22 **Five Minutes, Bunker Road**
The Baker-Barry Tunnel, built in 1918 and later enlarged, was used to haul guns and other supplies to Fort Barry. Traffic on the one lane road through the tunnel changes direction every five minutes.

PLATE 23 **Mirror Image, Larkspur Trestle**
The trestle, located off Highway 101 in Larkspur, serves no function since trains stopped coming to Marin. There is a proposal to have the structure removed and a parking lot installed. The town was mistakenly named after a flower thought to be a larkspur; in actuality it was a lupine.

PLATE 24 **Fountain, Plaza Vina del Mar**
This public garden in Sausalito's downtown historic district was named to honor its sister city in Chile. The fountain was designed for the Panama Pacific International Exposition held in San Francisco in 1915.

PLATE 25 **Spillway, Alpine Dam**
Located on the Fairfax-Bolinas Road, Alpine dam was constructed during World War I. Labor was scarce, but many Italian immigrants settled in the area and worked on the project. Its unique design is reminiscent of an ancient amphitheatre.

PLATE 26 **Sunlight, Muir Woods**
A water company threatened to condemn this canyon of redwoods by flooding it to make a reservoir. To save the trees, William Kent bought the property and presented it as a gift to President Theodore Roosevelt in 1908. Named for the naturalist John Muir, this national monument contains specimen trees 240 feet tall and a thousand years old.

PLATE 27 **Sawmill, Old Mill Park**
John Reed was awarded the first Mexican land grant in Marin in 1834. With the building of the sawmill on Cascade Creek in Mill Valley, this native of Ireland established the first commercial enterprise in the area.

PLATE 28 **Autumn Leaves, Camp Bothin**
Tamarancho and the Bothin Youth Center, which includes Arequipa, are part of the many acres northwest of Fairfax that are preserved as open space for the Girl Scouts and Boy Scouts.

PLATE 29 **Campsite, Samuel P. Taylor Park**
This state park near Lagunitas was originally called Taylorville for Samuel Penfield Taylor, a 49'er from New York. In 1856 he built the Pacific Coast's first paper mill. Surprisingly, the production of five tons of paper a day came from jute and old rags, and not from the nearby redwood trees.

PLATE 30 **Snow 2001, Mountain Theatre**
Snow on Mount Tamalpais is a rare sight, but reportedly four feet of snow fell here in 1922. Built in the 1930's by the Civilian Conservation Corps, this natural amphitheatre seats 4,000. Each stone within the 40 rows weighs an average of 1,500 pounds. It is the home of the annual Mountain Play.

PLATE 31 **Last Stop, West Point Inn**
Built in 1904, the West Point Inn marked the westernmost point of the Mount Tamalpais and Muir Woods Railway. Rooms rented for one dollar a night, less for the bunk beds. Famous for its lemonade and pancake breakfasts, the West Point Inn serves today as a respite for hikers and bikers.

PLATE 32 **Winter Picnic, Mount Tamalpais**
A mere 2,571 feet high, Mount Tamalpais, when viewed as a reclining figure, is sometimes referred to as the "sleeping maiden". The hundreds of hiking paths were originally created by animals traveling to their watering holes.

PLATE 33 **Shibui, Mount Tamalpais**
This view of the mountain is seen from the city of San Rafael. On a clear day, from the fire lookout station on top of Mount Tamalpais, one can see Mount Helena to the north, the Sierra Nevada to the east, and Mount Hamilton to the south.

PLATE 34 **Stranded, Tennessee Valley Cove**
This beach is named after the steamship *S.S. Tennessee* that broke apart when it missed the entrance to the harbor because of dense fog. The 500 passengers and the 14 chests of gold were miraculously rescued before the vessel became buried in the sand. It was not until 130 years later, in 1981, that the wreckage was uncovered.

PLATE 35 **Vanishing Point, China Camp**
After the 1906 earthquake, thousands of Chinese refugees are believed to have lived along the shores of San Pablo Bay. Now part of a 1,476-acre state park, there are still remnants of China Camp's historic past. A rickety wooden pier, a few weather-beaten buildings, and rusting fishing boats recall a bygone era.

PLATE 36 **Raven in Silhouette, Inverness**
Inverness, situated on Tomales Bay, was established by the Shafter family who named it after their ancestral home in Scotland. Street names such as Argyle, Dundee, and Aberdeen are reminders of their roots.

PLATE 37 **Stone Steps, Old St. Hilary**
St. Hilary's Church was built on a hill in Tiburon in 1888. It met the spiritual needs of the railroad workers who patronized the saloons on the main street below. Although it is no longer used for regular services, it is a favorite place for weddings.

PLATE 38 **Gazebo, Marin Art and Garden Center**
This former estate, located in the town of Ross, includes beautiful gardens and magnificent old trees. A non-profit group bought the land in 1945 and created an art gallery, a theatre, and a children's playground. It is also home to the Marin Society of Artists.

PLATE 39 **Lyford House, Tiburon**
This Victorian landmark, now home to the Richardson Bay Audubon Center, was barged a half mile across the bay from Strawberry Point to its present site in 1957. Dr. Benjamin Lyford, a former Civil War embalming surgeon, was in search of the fountain of youth when he promoted the area as a health resort. He refused to sell land to persons who drank, smoked, or kissed in public.

PLATE 40 **Stone Arch, Montgomery Chapel**
Located in San Anselmo, Montgomery Chapel is part of the San Francisco Theological Seminary. The Chapel has been used for weddings, bar mitzvahs, and as a recording studio for the rock star Van Morrison. Built in the 1890's, this style of architecture with its turrets and arches is called "Richarsonian Romanesque".

PLATE 41 **The Castle, San Anselmo**
The San Francisco Theological Seminary looms over the town of San Anselmo like a medieval castle. Construction began in 1892 when the stonemasons used hand-cut blue stone quarried in San

Rafael. Dr. William Anderson Scott originally established this church in a wild frontier town known as San Francisco, but he was driven out and hanged in effigy.

PLATE 42 Ivy Wall, The Seminary
On the Seminary's 21-acre campus in San Anselmo there are quiet places for study. "The Hub," an intersection where five streets come together with a total of 24 lanes of traffic, seems far away. San Anselmo was once called the Hub of Marin because it was a railroad junction along the line from Sausalito to Tomales with a spur track leading into San Rafael.

PLATE 43 Dunphy Park, Sausalito
Earl F. Dunphy Park, named after a former mayor, is home to this gazebo built to commemorate the United States Bicentennial. This town's most infamous mayor, Sally Stanford, once a bootlegger and a madam, is also part of the Sausalito's colorful past and has a street named after her.

PLATE 44 Garden Gate, Robson-Harrington Park
In 1910 a lumber magnate built a seventeen-room home on a three-acre estate in San Anselmo. This park, donated to the town, is known for its unusual walls made of brick salvaged from San Francisco after the 1906 earthquake and fire.

PLATE 45 671 Steps, Dipsea Trail
The second oldest foot race in the United States begins in the town of Mill Valley. The path travels 7.1 cross-country miles over Mount Tamalpais to Stinson Beach and starts with a climb up 671 steps. One of the steepest hills is known as Cardiac Arrest.

PLATE 46 Inkwells, Lagunitas
The Inkwells have long been a favorite swimming spot. Located on Paper Mill Creek near the entrance to Samuel P. Taylor State Park, these falls disappear as summer ends. In 2002 Coho salmon spawned in record numbers in creeks in the San Geromino Valley.

PLATE 47 Log Shelter, Phoenix Lake
Phoenix Lake, situated in Ross, is one of the seven lakes in the county belonging to the Marin Municipal Water District. Since it is a reservoir, no boating or swimming is permitted, but the California Department of Fish and Game stocks the lake for fishermen. A trail around the lake is popular with hikers and joggers.

PLATE 48 Glenwood Bridge, Ross
The town of Ross, known for its exclusive estates and beautiful homes, is very zealous about protecting its mature landscape. The first town council meeting, held in 1908, made it illegal to cut down any tree without permission. It is also against the law to tether a horse to a shade or ornamental tree. The town is unique in that it has no mail delivery.

PLATE 49 Falkirk, Mansion Row
Mission Avenue in San Rafael was home to many elegant estates. Falkirk, built in 1889, belonged to Captain Robert Dollar, owner of an international steamship line. The seventeen-room mansion built in the Queen Anne style is used today for art exhibits and cultural events. It also houses the Marin Poetry Center.

PLATE 50 Three Crosses, Mission San Rafael
Mission San Rafael was initially built in1817 and was used as a sanatorium for the mission Indians. St. Rafael's Church and a replica of the mission now occupy the site. Since the original architectural plans were never found, the mission's design was based on the style and spirit of the era.

PLATE 51 Palm Trees, St. Vincent
St. Vincent's School for Boys, located in north San Rafael, with its chapel, courtyards and archways has a European flavor. In the last 100 years, more than 50,000 boys have boarded there.

PLATE 52 Cinema, Fairfax
Motion picture companies used the hills of Fairfax as a backdrop for cowboy movies. This town was named after Lord Charles Snowden Fairfax from Virginia who was known for his gentlemanly conduct, even when gambling and drinking. One of the last fatal pistol duels in California took place in this town.

PLATE 53 Old Town, Novato
This historic downtown area in Novato, located at the east end of Grant Avenue around the old train depot, was originally called "New Town". Fires have destroyed many of the old buildings in this part of town.

PLATE 54 **County Line, Petaluma River Bridge**
The Petaluma River marks the Marin-Sonoma border. This tidal estuary was called a creek until an Act of Congress in 1959 changed it to a river. The northernmost community of Black Point was a major shipping station for lumber and livestock. Freight trains used the Northwestern Pacific track and Petaluma River Bridge to transport these goods.

PLATE 55 **Marin County Civic Center, San Rafael**
The Marin Civic Center was designed by the famous architect Frank Lloyd Wright who died before his project was built. Two main horizontal buildings were constructed to bridge four knolls; this was accomplished by creating wide arches over the roadways. The 172-foot aluminum spire conceals a smokestack to vent the cooling system.

PLATE 56 **Siesta, Hamilton Field**
Hamilton Field is the site of a former military installation built in 1935. It was a bomber and fighter base during World War II, and later became part of the United States Air Force Aerospace Defense Command. The area is now being developed as a residential community. The ubiquitous deer are fond of virtually everything edible planted by Marin's gardeners.

PLATE 57 **Fallen Oak, Buck Center**
Beryl Buck, a Ross widow who died in 1975, specified in her will that her 250 million dollar oil fortune be used to benefit the people of Marin County. The Buck Center, built high on a hill near Mount Burdell in Novato, was designed by the renowned architect I.M. Pei. It is used for biomedical research and education on aging.

PLATE 58 **Driving Range at Dusk, McInnis Park**
At the mouth of Las Gallinas Creek in San Rafael, McInnis Park is dedicated to the preservation of marsh, delta, and open space. The 450 acres include soccer fields, tennis courts, a canoe launch and a golf driving range. Bird watching is also a popular activity.

PLATE 59 **Last Standing Gate, Olompali**
Olompali, a state historic park two miles north of Novato, is on a site that was occupied by the Miwoks as early as the 1300's. The son of a village leader, Camillo Ynitia, was the only Native American in Marin to receive a Mexican land grant.

PLATE 60 **After the Harvest, West Marin**
Grape growing and winemaking originated in this county with the Spanish padres in the 1800's. It is now a developing industry in West Marin as dairy farmers begin to diversify. The moderate climate can be ideal, but deer and birds create problems for the growers.

PLATE 61 **Iron Pot, Olompali**
Called a try pot, this cast iron kettle was used by the Miwoks for rendering tallow from cattle they raised. Try pots were originally manufactured for use on whaling ships.

PLATE 62 **Lone Oak, Ignacio**
The coastal live oak, tanoak, and scrub oak have always been a part of the Marin landscape, but thousands have been felled in recent years by Sudden Oak Death. The fungus, first detected in a tanoak in 1995 in Mill Valley, has also spread to bay laurel and California buckeye.

PLATE 63 **Downtown, Nicasio**
A once bustling community, this town now seems frozen in time. Ranching, dairying, and logging of redwoods kept the residents busy, but the lack of a harbor and the failure of the railroad to reach Nicasio kept it isolated and rural.

PLATE 64 **Three Cows, Hicks Valley**
Dairy and cattle ranchers live in this pastoral setting in Hicks Valley. William Hicks was an absentee landlord from Tennessee who arrived in 1843 and amassed a land empire that stretched over five counties.

PLATE 65 **Paradise, Blackie's Pasture**
The statue of Blackie is a landmark in Tiburon. The old swaybacked horse grazed here for a quarter of a century, and when he died in 1966 at age 40, he was buried on this site. From this point there is a two-mile path into the town along a railroad right-of-way.

PLATE 66 **Windmill, Chileno Valley**
This valley west of Novato is ranching country. It was named for a colony of Chilean-born residents who arrived here in the 1860's.

PLATE 67 **Maine Street, Tomales**
The oldest church in Marin County, built in 1860, is an example of "Carpenter Gothic" architecture. The original settlement in Tomales was called Lower Town, but silting prevented shipping on the creek so it faded from existence. Luther Burbank lived here for a short time and developed a potato that he called "Bodega Red".

PLATE 68 **Shadows, Point Reyes-Petaluma Road**
The Marin French Cheese Factory, located in Hicks Valley, was founded in 1865. It is famous for its Camembert and Brie cheeses that are made on the premises. The park-like setting is a favorite spot for picnics.

PLATE 69 **Escalle, Magnolia Avenue**
French-born Jean Escalle was one of the early successful winemakers in Marin until prohibition and plant lice wiped out production. This building, located in Larkspur and identified by its red color, was called the Limerick Inn. Customers arrived by train to listen to a band and play bocce ball.

PLATE 70 **Wooden Arbor, Green Gulch**
Located near Muir Beach in a tranquil valley, Green Gulch Farm offers retreats and studies in Zen Buddhism. There is also a working organic farm and herb garden on the property.

PLATE 71 **Clasped Hands, Horseshoe Hill**
The oldest cemetery in Marin was necessitated by a dramatic rise in deaths as a result of a smallpox epidemic in1853. During the gold rush, Bolinas swelled to 40,000 residents, many of whom were employed in the lumber industry to meet the needs of the rapidly expanding city of San Francisco.

PLATE 72 **Meditating Angel, Bolinas**
The angel is located in the Mary Magdalene portion of the cemetery in Bolinas. Mexican land grant owners, the Briones, originally used the land as a cow pasture.

PLATE 73 **Morning Mist, Marinwood**
This grove is part of 317 acres of land donated to the Roman Catholic Church in 1853 to establish St. Vincent's School near Marinwood. The school was originally used to house six orphaned girls but within a year they were replaced by boys.

PLATE 74 **Elephant Rocks, Dillon Beach Road**
These natural landmarks were carved out through centuries of erosion caused by wind and rain. They can be viewed on the road to Dillon Beach.

PLATE 75 **White Fence, Dillon Beach**
Named after an Irish pioneer, Dillon Beach on Bodega Bay has been a popular resort community for years. Seeking relief from summer heat, visitors come here to be cooled by the fog that rolls in almost every day. The Russians, who arrived in the early 1800's to trap sea otters, called the area Point Romanzov.

PLATE 76 **Solitude, Nicasio Reservoir**
It was necessary to flood several ranches in order to construct Nicasio Reservoir in 1960. Lake Lagunitas, built in 1872, is the oldest and the smallest of the reservoirs. Kent, created in 1953, is the largest and Soulajule, built in 1979, is the newest.

PLATE 77 **Journey, St. Vincent Drive**
The eucalyptus trees that cover the Marin landscape were brought from Australia by the gold seekers. Homesick, the men planted seedlings on the barren hillsides to replicate what they had left behind. Unchecked growth and their potential for fire have made the trees unpopular. In Australia they are called widow makers because their branches break suddenly without warning.

PLATE 78 **Six Curlews, Seadrift**
These shorebirds are a familiar sight at dusk, but the appearance of thousands of jellyfish covering Stinson Beach is a rare occurrence. Known as by-the-wind-sailors, these jellyfish are related to the Portuguese man-of-war. They appear in the spring when the northwest winds blow and can look like an oil spill on the surface of the water.

PLATE 79 **Lifeguard Station, Stinson Beach**
Stinson Beach was originally called Easkoot's Beach in the 1880's. Captain Easkoot, who ran a tent camp, was known to fire a shotgun to discourage beachcombers from removing driftwood. Now the bathers' concern is for the occasional shark.

PLATE 80 **Low Tide, Tomales Bay**
Since the San Andreas Fault runs directly beneath the shallow water of Tomales Bay, it is sometimes called "Earthquake Bay". San Franciscans were drawn to this quiet corner of the world after the 1906 earthquake thinking they were far removed from its epicenter. The bay is twelve and a half miles long.

PLATE 81 **Boat Dock, Bolinas Lagoon**
Bolinas Lagoon sustains large numbers of migratory birds. A recently sighted greater sand plover is the first of its kind ever recorded in the western hemisphere. Environmentalists and engineers are currently debating whether increasing sediment will result in this shallow estuary's becoming a meadow.

PLATE 82 **Promontory, Point Reyes Lighthouse**
From the Point Reyes Lighthouse, gray whales can be seen during the winter months migrating from the Bering Sea to Baja, California. The rocky shelves below are home to common murres and sea lions. The lighthouse was built in 1870.

PLATE 83 **Circle of Boats, Marshall**
Located on Highway One, the town of Marshall is named after five Irish brothers. In 1913 the inventor of the radio, Guglielmo Marconi, planned to link the globe with wireless transmitters. Marshall became the main west coast site for broadcasting to Hawaii.

PLATE 84 **Tower, Point Reyes Lighthouse**
Official records show this area to be the second foggiest spot on the North American continent and the windiest place on the Pacific Coast. Equipped with a Fresnel lens, the lighthouse casts a rotating beam that can be seen for 24 nautical miles.

PLATE 85 **Cottage, Cypress Grove**
Surrounded by tall cypress trees, Cypress Grove Preserve north of Marshall was donated to the Audubon Canyon Ranch for nature studies. The property has also been used as a poultry farm, a chinchilla farm, and a box factory.

PLATE 86 **Oyster Beds, Tomales Bay**
Oysters have been cultivated in Tomales Bay since 1875 when seventeen freight cars arrived with East Coast oysters to be planted in the tidelands. Fences were built in the water to protect the beds from predators.

PLATE 87 **Lifeboat Station, Chimney Rock**
This lifesaving station at Point Reyes was established in 1890 because of the numerous shipwrecks that plagued the Pacific Coast. Men walked the beaches in four-hour shifts searching for survivors. The station is named for the huge sea stack that marks the entrance to Drake's Bay. Some historians believe the explorer Sir Francis Drake landed here in 1579 with his ship, the *Golden Hind*.

PLATE 88 **Late Afternoon, Pierce Point Ranch**
At the northern tip of the Point Reyes Peninsula, the Pierce family ran a model dairy ranch. In the 1880's making butter was a major industry in this area. Now the major attraction is the tule elk brought here to replace native herds that roamed freely 140 years ago.

PLATE 89 **Three Trees, Limantour Estuary**
The estero, Spanish for estuary, is located at Point Reyes and is a popular place for bird watching. Mudflats provide food and refuge for many species of birds including egrets, herons, and cormorants. A colony of seals makes itself at home on the sandbars.

PLATE 90 **Day's End, Mount Tamalpais**
Mount Tamalpais is the focal point of the county which was established in 1850 in the new state of California. The origin of the name, Marin, is somewhat vague. According to Louise Teather in *Place Names of Marin*… "the name …honoring a legendary Indian who was either a great chief or a skilled sailor, or one and then the other; or recalling a Spanish name given during the first charting of the Bay in 1775; or all of the above."

BIBLIOGRAPHY

Arrigoni, Patricia, *Making the Most of Marin*. Presidio Press, Novato, California, 1981.

Futcher, Jane, *Marin, The Place, The People*. Holt, Rinehart and Winston, New York, New York 1981.

Keegan, Frank L. *San Rafael, Marin's Mission City*. Windsor Publications, Inc. Northridge, California, 1987.

Mason, Jack, *The Making of Marin*. North Shore Books, Inverness, California, 1975.

Teather, Louise, *Discovering Marin*. The Tamal Land Press, Fairfax, California, 1974.

Teather, Louise, *Place Names of Marin*. Scottwall Associates, San Francisco, California, 1986.

Tracy, Jack, *Sausalito, Moments in Time*. Windgate Press, Sausalito, California, 1983.

ABOUT THE ARTISTS

GLYNIS MARIANI is a freelance photographer whose work has appeared in local newspapers including the Pacific Sun. She grew up in Marin County exploring the diverse beauty of the landscape, from the trails of Mount Tamalpais to the beaches of West Marin. Glynis has been a photography instructor for 10 years and is inspired by sharing her love of nature and her passion for photography with others.

BEV SCHNEIR has been involved with the photography community in Marin for many years. Winner of local and national photo contests, she has been published in Photographer's Forum and has exhibited at galleries in Marin and the Design Center in San Francisco. Bev has been a resident of Marin for 30 years and hikes many miles each week, and always with her camera.

ACKNOWLEDGMENTS

We are sincerely grateful to Michael Kenna for his inspiration and guidance; Isabel Allende for revealing her very personal connection to Marin; Deirdre Sharett for finding the poetic and lyrical words to accompany our images; Lise Stampfli Torme for her skill and dedication in designing this book; and Ken Coburn of Global Interprint, Inc. for his advice and direction in printing this book. We also wish to thank Paul Fusco for his incisive critique of our portfolio and Martin Cruz Smith, Beth Ashley, Michael Krasny, and Lee Sankowich for their generous comments.

GLYNIS MARIANI & BEV SCHNEIR

I offer my love and gratitude to the people in my life who have supported me on my visual journey and throughout this project: my husband Dave whose knowledge of Marin County and ability to open doors were invaluable; my children Jenica, Dave, and Sara for their understanding and patience even when it meant another pizza for dinner; my mother Dede for her insight and wisdom during the countless hours over the many months; my father Paul for his unwavering belief in me; and Pat Fusco for her gift of time and expertise on the longest day. I am also indebted to the teachers who have graced my life with their vision and the students who have allowed me to share my vision with them.

GLYNIS MARIANI

I would like to express my appreciation to my family and friends for their continuous support and encouragement while I worked on this project: my husband Hal who has been my camera "sherpa" for many years and many miles; my son Jeremy and daughter Rebecca who, on leaving for college, told me to "get a life"; Toby Scott, the first to mat, frame, and actually hang one of my photos in her home; Leigh Abell, darkroom architect, and the Marin Photography Club where I learned not only to look but "to see"; Asher Rubin, grammarian extraordinaire; Sandy Bienstock, location scout; the hiking group led by Carolyn Coogan who listened to me every Friday, and Barbara Madland who listened to me the other six days.

BEV SCHNEIR